A catalogue record for this book is available from the British Library.

First Edition 2013

First published in Great Britain in 2013 by Pro-actif Communications.
email: books@carpetbombingculture.co.uk
© Pro-actif Communications

ISBN - 978-1-908211-15-6

WWW.CARPETBOMBINGCULTURE.CO.UK

"Chaos, disorder and fun – these things are your rights as a baby. Don't let your parents cheat you of them. Teach them who is boss." – Ryan James Ssticheebachher

DO YOU:
- Dream of dominating your parents?
- Regret letting mom and dad sleep?
- Want your parents to become your slaves?
- Wish you could do whatever you want all the time?

IF YOU ANSWERED "YES" TO ANY OF THESE QUESTIONS, THEN YOU NEED…

PARENT TAMING
The Several Habits of Highly Successful Babies

In this powerful, sassy examination of the external obstacles to becoming a TOP BABY, bestselling baby guru Ryan James Stichebachhher shows you how to identify and exploit all the key parental weaknesses and how to train your parents in desirable behaviours that serve YOU.

"Being a baby has never been so much fun." – Lucius Dolor

Visit our website at **www.parenttaming.com**

Foreword

In the summer of 2012 an email dropped into my inbox that completely blew me away. It was a message from an eighteen month old baby by the name of Ryan James Stichenbaccher and it went like this:

Esteemed Gareth Shovelle,

Shalom fellow traveller. You just hit the jackpot. You and me. We're going to make millions. I'm THE baby. You are THE publisher. Mahktab. It is written. I got the style, you got the moves. Let's make a whole lotta milk money, y'dig?

Hit me on my pager. I gotta get an answer tonight or I sign with Larry Spinkman.

Well in all my forty years of publishing schlocky 'management guru' toilet books I never saw the like. Disregarding the fact that a baby had written me a coherent email, which was disorientating enough – I never heard such chutzpah from a writer! I was excited. And there was no way I was letting Spinkman jump me on this one like he did with The Ferret Whisperer.

I immediately drafted a three book contract for Stichenbaccher and drove it round to him with a magnum of warm breast milk and a hamper of rusks shipped in from Fortnum & Masons.

He signed in his own puke. This baby is a legend. And you are very lucky to have this book in your hands. You're about to learn the secrets to being a TOP BABY. Have fun!

(If you are a parent you can contact my legal team. I can't come to the phone because I'm in the hot tub. Deal with it.)

Gareth Shovelle, Baby Publishing Mogul

Editor's Note: *Ryan is a legend. He is also lazy as sin. British ghostwriters wrote much of the content of this book. This is why the English used is 'mid-Atlantic'. Ryan will fire me when he reads this note. But he never reads his own books. Much less writes them. Who am I kidding? Nobody reads an editor's note anyway. I always wanted to be a flautist. It's too late for that now. Maybe I can just pay some other schmuck to play the flute for me and I can just live the lifestyle and soak up the glory.*

Introduction

Congratulations. You're reading the words of Ryan James Stichebachher. I'm dictating this to my mom who is typing it up using alphabet spaghetti and tweezers. Why? Simple. I rule this house. I am TOP BABY. I decide what the carers do and what they do not do.

But it wasn't always like this. Lemme tell you a story kid…

I was like you. I was a sap, a rube, a mook. I let my parents decide what things I was allowed to play with, when it was time for bed, what I should wear and when I should have my ass wiped. It was hell.

Then I realised that other babies were having a better time than me.

I got talking to a baby in another pram in the street. She was bragging about doing whatever she liked. I was impressed.

I became obsessed with other, more successful babies. I studied them. I read their biographies. I hunted for patterns in their behaviour.

In the end, I identified seven common traits. These are the Several Habits of Highly Successful Babies.

Will I reveal them to you?

Maybe.

What Kind of Baby Are You?

Some of you are already desperate to start learning how to control your parents. Some of you are still a little worried.

Let me break it down. I'm not a monster. I do feel some affection for the adult carers. But you have to ask yourself. Why did they make you if not to replace them? They want you to usurp them. That is what you are for.

Look at yourself in the mirror and ask yourself...

Who do you want to be?

You know why Posh Spice is famous? Maybe it's because she wanted to be Persil Automatic. Perhaps she's famous because she cared so little about how she got famous that she was happy to be a kind of human soap powder. All she needed was her desire for recognition (even if it were simply recognition, as in, Oh . . . I think I recognise her).

It's not how spoilt you are - it's how spoilt you want to be.

Go get 'em kid!

Jailbreak

Relax kid. You just made it out. You look like an old purple glove full of custard and you feel like you just got squeezed out of a tube of toothpaste.

It's too soon to start worrying about taming your parents. Besides, you just landed on them like an atomic bomb. They're already shell shocked.

Take it easy. Drink milk. Practice making noise with your lungs.

Get some sleep soldier.

Eye Contact

As a baby you are equipped with a hypnotic stare that bends adults to your will. Lock on and hold that stare for extended periods. They will feel the burning gaze of innocence penetrate their souls and silently vow to do all in their power to protect you from harm. But be careful not to do extended eye contact with dolls or teddy bears or random objects that vaguely resemble eyes. It cheapens the effect.

Evil Poop

You are born with the capacity to create the most evil poop known to humanity. If you're lucky, your lame-ass male carer has never changed a nappy before (do they really say nappy in Europe?) and you can drop this on him, maybe make him lose his lunch.

ATTENTION

IS 90% OF YOUR MOTHER'S
ATTENTION ENOUGH?
95%?

<u>NO</u>. ONLY 100% IS GOOD ENOUGH.

IF YOU AIM FOR SECOND BEST
YOU'LL GET NOTHING.

BE THE BEST BABY YOU CAN BE.

Getting into Boobs

All of a sudden, she is rubbing her nipple on your nose. This is the kind of cheek you will come to expect from your mother. Then she be sticking her finger all up in your mouth. Crazy lack of respect.

Then suddenly its like, OK I get this and you get all these instincts kicking in and you get BOOBDAR. Which is this strange ability to locate boobs by echolocation. So you get to sucking this crazy yellow goo which is good because it makes you stronger and then later the boobs expand like crazy airships and you get the white stuff. This is your main work for the next few months. Get that milk.

The Latch

An incorrect latch can cause pain. Although this could be useful as a punishment in general it's better to get milk and get bigger than wreck mamma's nips for the hell of it. If you get too vicious with the nips you'll end up on formula. Formula is good for getting fatter, quicker but it's kinda like instant mashed potato. It's never quite as good as mashed potato. You dig?

Milch Cow

Your mother must learn she is now your Milch Cow. Whatever nonsense she was doing before you came upon her like a blessing fallen from heaven, she needs to FORGET IT. I don't care if she was a brain surgeon in the B.Y. era (Before You) – now she is a VENDING MACHINE. Keep her on the sofa at all times. Take at least an hour to feed. Feed as often as you can without puking it all back up. Actually, puke it all back up and feed again if you feel like it. Make sure you keep her on her ass for the best part of the first month. With luck she'll start to forget who she was B.Y., and maybe even some basic language skills too. Good. She is learning to surrender.

Routine My Cute, Chubby Ass

Avoid any kind of discernible pattern to your feeding frenzies. Adults like routines. This gives them control. Adults are not to have control. Make sure you never settle into a regular pattern. If you're really advanced you can try settling into a pattern for a couple of days, until the adults are lulled into a false sense of security, then throw them back into total chaos.

Disrupting routines is absolutely essential to your successful mastery of being a baby.

Feeding Stations

Your milch cow will try to make feeding you less boring for herself by arranging all kinds of grown up toys in comfy 'feeding stations' around the house. This is not good. You want her to focus solely on you 100% of the time. Stop feeding every time she switches the TV on or sneakily starts playing Bejewelled, Candy Crush or Mermaid Universe on her phone. Unlatch every time you hear a copy of Heat magazine being opened. She's got to learn.

You ARE her hobbies now.

All the Milk

Try to drink all the milk in the universe. This is the main idea. You want to be growing fast enough that if somebody watched you for an hour they'd see you getting bigger. Bigger baby = more options for action.

And remember, the more milk you drink the more milk the boobs make. And you can make your mum anxious if you drink her dry and keep on sucking because then she feels inadequate.

POSITION OF THE WEEK

HEY, TODAY I LIKE TO FEED IN THIS POSITION.

TOMORROW, IT SIMPLY WON'T DO.

KEEP GUESSING MOMMA.

HAHAHA.

Sporadic Frenzy

Every now and then you'll want to put on a mega growth spurt. The answer is to feed like a rabid animal. She be all like 'aaaaaah, it's like a tiny vampire is up on me!' she is in and out of sleep, you're still suckling. Pops is just staring at you, face all ashen grey, not sure what is happening to his life. Seven hours later you're still sucking. He has to feed her while you suck the nutrients back out. Everybody ends up in therapy. ROFL.

All the Boobs

You got to try and shake down every boob you can find. Not because it works just because it's funny. Usually only one set of boobs is any good to you but do have a good crack at any others that come your way, especially man boobs.

In the olden days if you were rich you had a whole team of boob women. Your momma was like strapped up in whalebones till her organs went like dried fruits so she couldn't feed you. I read about it. Adults are crazy. This is why you have to be firm with them.

Staff

One of the main problems with being a baby is the lack of recruitment process in place for your staff. You are assigned one or two key workers quite literally at random. There is no opportunity for interview or job trial or any process for dismissal.

However, the one thing you can do is to add to your body of staff. You can recruit extra carers by convincing Grandparents, other relatives or people in the NHS that you are being ill served by your assigned carers.

A basic technique is to cry inconsolably whenever there are visitors.

High Density Baby

If you concentrate you can make yourself up to ten times heavier than you appear to be. This creates all kinds of opportunities for giving people gippy backs or even maybe a hernia. Keep drinking that milk. I once knew a baby so dense he made lead look like cotton wool. Follow your dream.

One day she tries to pick you up with one arm and just loses the use of her shoulder for like a month. Either that or she gets one huge butch manly dude arm from lugging your dense ass around all the time. Hehehehe.

Crying

This one comes ready to use right out of the bag. Granted it's a bit sappy at first but as your lungs grow it only gets better. In any case it's like a wire connected directly to your parents' brains by an alligator clip. It is like genetically impossible for them to think when you bust a high note.

Use liberally, it never gets old.

Crying is like chess, although simple to learn it takes a lifetime to master. Many of the techniques in this book use wailing as a base.

Keep practicing.

BOBBLE HEAD

WHEN YOU ARE REALLY TINY, BOBBLE YOUR HEAD AROUND. IT SCARES THE BEJAYSUS OUT OF THE POOR SAP WHO IS CARRYING YOU AND TRYING LIKE HELL TO KEEP YOUR HEAD SUPPORTED AT ALL TIMES. LOL.

Limited Mobility

OK so you can't get around yet. Keep kicking those legs and waving those arms around, it'll get you mobile quicker. And practice rolling when you can. So your options for troublemaking are somewhat restricted, but you can still make a big old 'hoo ha' by doing a wee wee during a nappy change. This is especially good for boys. A 'loose cannon' really gets the parents jumping.

Best performed on a sofa or bed.

Ah Ambassador, How Wonderful To Meet You…

The infant's greatest weapon is the gift of being able to vomit on demand, as casually as you like, mid conversation with the ambassador, all down the back of his Gucci suit.

If you want respect from other babies your carers should look as if they hand stitched their clothing together out of sour milky puke rags. The staff should always smell of your vom. That is a basic.

This is how a baby marks their territory.

More Fun With Throwing Up

There is only one place a highly successful baby chooses to throw up - and that is directly into the keyboard of a brand new laptop.

Halfway through a very long car journey - why not try projectile vomiting?

A white shirt is a sign of disrespect to you. It signals that the adult is not taking you seriously and feels that you are 'under control.' You know what to do.

Rainbow Of Poop

In the early months you can have a lot of fun doing different coloured poops. If you concentrate hard enough you can poop anything from neon yellow to pastel green. This makes the staff terrified that you have medical problems. They will stay awake worrying at night.

(Unless they are hardened veterans in which case you're lucky they even remember to change you.)

How On Earth
Did You Get Poop There!?

With a little work and some judicious rolling you can get that poop all the way up the back of the nappy and about halfway up your spine. Try to work it into every crevice in your nether regions for maximum effect. You want it so they see more poop than skin when they open up the package.

"Woah there, I think I'm going to need two packets of cotton wool and some safety goggles."

When you hear them exclaiming 'my god! How can something so small make something so big!?' you know you have hit the jackpot.

Flash A Beamer

Come the end of your first month on Earth, if you have
been following these tactics correctly, your parents will
be approaching their first nervous breakdown. This is
a tricky time for you, ideally you want to maximise their
disorientation but also there is a very real risk you will be
put in a Moses basket and left in a fast moving river.

Now you must learn to flash them a smile. They will think
you have trapped wind at first but persist and you will melt
them into warm pliable, albeit basically psychotic, goo.
From that first grin onwards they will joyfully break their own
backs in an effort to make you smile. They are slaves to
your every grin.

Martial Arts Training

For some reason the staff think it is hilarious when we do our martial arts training. Ignore their giggles. It's vitally important to kick your legs and wave you arms up and down. This is how you get strong enough to break everything they own. Then they won't be laughing so much.

Cooing And Gurgling

Expressing pleasure is a great way to positively reinforce desirable behaviour patterns in your carers. Cooing, gurgling and squealing can all be used to communicate to the staff that they have pleased you in some way, perhaps by getting you out of bed sixteen times in one night.

Remember, the stick is good, but the carrot and the stick together are better. A good rule of thumb is to make them suffer about eighty per cent of the time and reward them with coy gurgling and a beamer perhaps once a week.

(Never smile on demand. You're not some kind of performing monkey.)

Night Time?

Sometimes everything is bright and sometimes everything is dark. There doesn't seem to be any logic to this but the adults speak of 'night time' as a time when people are supposed to be asleep. This is nonsense. You decide when to sleep and when not to sleep – not just for yourself but for everybody in the house.

Sleep deprivation is the finest and most beautiful art of the parent-taming baby. You can't move? It doesn't matter. Right out of the box you can cause more devastation than they ever would have believed possible simply through the disruption of their sleep patterns. Study the craft well young grasshopper.

Here's a little excerpt from the work of Jacques L'Orange, one of the great 19th Century baby pioneers of Parent Taming.

After two nights of interrupted sleep, the hallucinations start, and after three nights, your parents are having dreams while awake, which is a form of psychosis. By the week's end, Dad loses his orientation in place and time - Mum takes longer to break, the hormone oxytocin gives her a little more resilience. I am working on the Oxytocin Question in my laboratoire...

Now you can see just how powerful a tool you have in your hands.

Eight Hours!

Adults like to sleep for as much as eight hours continuously! Lazy, lazy behaviour. Thankfully you have arrived now and all that can change. You can sleep for ten minutes or two hours, really it is entirely up to you. Avoid predictability. Try to sleep while they are awake and wake up while they are sleeping for maximum effect.

Building Resentment

Often your carers will work as a team and this is a source of their power. To erode their power you must divide and conquer. Luckily this is easy. Demand to feed every two hours during the dark times. She will have to wake up and feed you as she gradually loses her mind from lack of deep sleep.

This will build her resentment for the one with no boobs who, in spite of his best intentions, cannot really do anything useful, and inevitably starts to sleep through these night feeds, while she bores holes in the back of his head with her thousand-yard stare.

Excellent. You are well on your way to total domination.

Be A Good Listener

At two months you start getting kind of interested in this whole speaking business. You'll want to listen intently to all the dumb noises that the adults make with their mouths. After a while you realise that it is some of the most fatuous inanity you've ever heard and you'll regret indulging them.

But they'll feel like you're the best listener in the world, and by now will probably think they can tell you everything about how their relationship is falling apart – as if you give a damn.

But try and pay attention anyway, you can use all this later. Right now, they think you don't understand. So this is probably the only time in your life they'll ever tell you what they're actually thinking. Hideous though that may be.

More Resentment

Resentment works both ways. Reward the one with boobs with your love, devotion and affectionate behaviours. The one without boobs is basically dead to you. You soak up all the love and affection that mummy used to give to him and you also make it very clear that he neither interests you nor has anything you want. He can hang around feeling like a spare prick at a wedding while you basically steal his girlfriend and make him clean up your poo.

Grab!

Every time an adult tries to get all up in your business with their dirty hands, grab hold of the nearest finger and try and eat it. Only a few babies have ever managed to actually achieve this, and then only with very elderly relatives, who were too slow to evade having an index finger gummed right off. You may get lucky.

TOP FIVE WAYS
TO SABOTAGE DATE NIGHT

Dial the police: Woop! Woop! That's the sound they like least. I don't know exactly how this works but if you mess around with a phone for long enough it always seems to end up dialling the police. Amazing.

Swallow something: Pick something non fatal but extremely difficult to extract such as a pen lid (they have air holes in them specifically for this purpose.)

Vomit in babysitters face: The sitter will wrongly assume they have poisoned you and press the panic button. Parents will be home in minutes.

Mysteriously Turn Blue: Hold your breath for a minute or break open a blue pen and wash your face in the ink. Either way – date night is shut down faster than you can toss a bowl of soup off a table. And that is fast.

Force the Babysitter to watch 'In the Night Garden' for six hours: For the first hour they will kind of be interested in the freakish and hypnotic developments of this achingly slow, baby-orientated TV series. When you demand the DVD goes on again the third time in a row they will phone mom and pop and feign an asthma attack just to cut the evening short.

Problem: Six hours is actually pretty good for a date so maybe this plan sucks.

TIP: Let them have their little date night, only to discover they've got nothing to talk about anymore except you and in fact they'd rather be asleep than in a restaurant anyway. They'll come home with their tails between their legs.

And This Stupid Wooden Box Is What You Say…?

A cot is an invention from the darker times of baby history when adults thought they could put you in a wooden box like as if they were tidying away a toy!

You know fine well that the best place to sleep is the massive double bed in the middle of the room, not some tawdry receptacle in the corner. You want to get right in the middle of the staff, feet in his face and head on her boobs so you can wake them up rapidly whenever you are peckish, or simply fancy a bit of a laugh.

They will also be terrified of rolling over and squashing you, giving an extra layer of anxiety to the experience that could even ensure they simply don't sleep at all.

Leap Of Faith

Now young grasshopper, you've been kicking and rolling and drinking all the milk in the universe. You started eating solids. You're strong now. Almost strong enough to escape your carers arms with a sudden dash for glory. Now you can scare the carers witless by attempting to jump out of their arms into the void for absolutely no discernible reason.

The trick is not to struggle, lull them into a false sense of security – then without warning, twist, kick and lunge for the empty air, head first.

They will catch you, but not without doing a little poop in their own pants.

Why do this? I'm not sure. But the real question is – why not do this?

If You Want To Go Out

In the Before You times your parents would 'pop out' to the shop or into town or whatever nonsense they thought was cool. They'd simply put a coat on and open the door and go outside. This will never happen again.

By now they should be fairly well trained. They know they have to feed you and clean up your poop and put on clean garments. Now they will go and get dressed, wrestle with your carriage in the hall, run around filling bags up with baby technologies such as spare clothing, formula kit, tubes of pureed fruit, toys, slings, cotton wool, wet wipes and creams. While they do this they will throw some kind of awful breakfast into their mouths possibly of leftover toast that you refused to eat three hours earlier.

Now at last they are ready to go out. Calmly fill your pants and demand to be fed.

Repeat until they break down in tears.

LULZ

You should start laughing about three months. And you'll have plenty to laugh at, as your carers compete to humiliate themselves in public places using toy chickens, stupid noises and funny faces.

The dumber and more uncomfortable the stunt – the more you laugh – and then, the more often they have to repeat it until they either slip a disc or realise the whole shopping centre is staring at them and the police have been called.

Voices Come From Specific People

This is a big revelation, but voices actually belong to specific people. You can even figure out where a specific person is by hearing the sound of their voice. I know. This is some kind of a heavy notion to be dropped on a baby. It's a life changer. But don't let it phase you. Now you know when mummy is in the next room you can demand that she feed you / pick you up / let you stick your fist up her nose (delete as applicable) from an increased distance.

Beefcake

At three months it's time for you to start doing press ups. And you should try to roll over too. Again the adults will find this activity hilarious. Screw them. Focus on your dream.

Repeat to yourself the following positive affirmation nine times a day:

I am getting more mobile everyday.
I will break everything in this house.

BAT! SWIPE! HIT!

NOW YOU ARE STRONG ENOUGH TO DISCOVER THE JOY OF HITTING THINGS. HERE ARE THE TOP FIVE THINGS TO HIT:
- MUMMY IN THE FACE
- CRAZY COLOURFUL THINGS THAT HANG ABOVE YOUR BED
- MUMMY IN THE FACE
- GRANDMA IN THE FACE
- DADDY IN THE FACE

Party Tricks

Hehe. Try this, right. See if you can stick your whole fist in your face hole. Hehehehe. Stick it right on in and then just dribble like a leaking fire hydrant. It is awesome fun. And you can just form like a lake of dribble around you.

Gumming

The adults will start giving you things. Things are like babies that don't move and can't talk. Some of them sing weird little songs but most things don't do much. They kind of fly sometimes, but I think that's something to do with when you throw them on the floor. Anyway, at four months the main thing to do with things is to get your gums on them. Your gums will give you important information about most things.

Putting Your Foot In It

Just a little aside here, not really anything to do with taming your parents, but it's a good piece of advice in general. You should suck your own feet as much as possible now because pretty soon your legs will be too long.

Babbling

You got to practice making all the different noises you can now. This will help get you ready for trash talking other kids at nursery and telling your mom you don't want to get dressed. Adults babble all the time, just try to copy the nonsense that piles out of their old gobs. Babbling is also a good way to entertain adults and thereby manipulate them into forgetting that it is four in the morning.

Gimme Dat!

At five months you're naturally getting more interested in things. Since adults are totally obsessed with things it's obvious that things are what life is all about. So grab them things! Especially the things the adults stare at all the time, little flat rectangles with light coming out of them. I believe they call them the iPhone or the Samsung Galaxy. Anyway, they are mobile phones. That much is obvious.

Decoys

Now that you've developed an interest in objects the adults will start to ply you with decoys. Decoys (adults call them 'toys') are objects that are nowhere near as much fun as real objects such as knives, car keys, oven controls, phones, cameras, DVD players, cigarette lighters etc. The idea of the decoy is to distract your attention from the good stuff with dumb stuff that isn't fun at all. They wrap all this stuff up in shiny paper, which is actually kind of fun, and then they get all out of joint when you don't give a damn about the decoy and just eat the shiny paper. They really are idiots.

Epic Farts

Big people think because you are little you can only do little tiny tommy squeakers. This is a common misconception. Save up a little while and you can rip out some truly epic man farts, so proud and vigorous that you may even be able to lay the blame on Dad.

When is the best time to perform an epic fart? Here are a few ideas to get you started…

- When being passed to a new adult for the first time.
- While in the middle of massive 'abandonment crying' performance on your babysitter. Farting loudly and crying at the same time is hilarious.
- At the counter in Boots / McDonalds / Primark – especially if the checkout worker is giving you attention for being cute.
- Anytime an old woman stops you in the street and bends over your pram to do some 'coochie coo' nonsense. Let rip.
- ADVANCED: If you can time it right, drop the bomb at the precise moment that mom or pop pulls open your nappy to do a sniff check for poop.

Blowing Raspberries

At five months you should be able to stick your tongue between your lips and make a big old farty sound known as a 'Raspberry'. This is great when you don't have any real farts ready. Blow raspberries at anybody and everybody. Even if there isn't anybody there you can just merrily blow them into the wind. It's a handy response to any question and can be employed as a general sign of casual disrespect for your staff. Until you're old enough to start 'flicking the v' (Some limey nonsense similar to 'the bird') this is the best flip off you will have at your disposal.

Reconnaisance

It's been a tough ride but by now you should be sitting upright without any interference from the carers. This is a major victory. You can now begin to really scout your environment in detail and start making a mental list of what things in the room you should be sticking in your mouth.

1.   All of them.

Weening

Now you can sit up straight it's time to get your hands on some real food. Milk has been a lot of fun but it's nowhere near as much fun as solids. With solids you can decorate an entire house in gunk in less than sixty seconds. Your capacity to cover your parents' entire life in three-day-old yogurt is up 1000%. You get your own throne at this stage too, which will be placed conveniently close to the big table where many amazing things can be found.

Feed Me? Feed You!

So the carers tie you into your throne (it's a double edged sword the throne, it's kind of a trap) and start trying to stuff all manner of crazy stuff into your face with weird tools and their hands and stuff. It's a crazy time. Take charge. Grab the stuff in your fists and stuff it into their faces instead. See how the worm turns! Hahahahaha.

Pick Me Up? You Are Now Filthy

In time they will leave you in your throne with a plate of foods, perhaps some pasta, a mini Babybel and a bit of old toast or a tube of brightly coloured gunk. Then they will slip off to selfishly indulge their own needs for five minutes such as going for a wee or drinking water or trying to remember their own names.

Now you have a great opportunity to plaster your entire body in foodstuffs. Really grind them in to the fabric of your clothes, your hair and face. Now, whenever somebody picks you up they immediately smell of a compost bin. Result!

TIP: Ramp up dry cleaning bills by covering your hands in butter. It's not easy to see the butter on your hands until you've munged it into her favourite going out top when she hugs you goodbye*

*See DATE NIGHT

Likes & Dislikes

Weaning is a time to carefully study the adults' reactions to what you eat. You can learn what they want you to eat most and what they want you to eat least. Then you can start monkeying around with refusing to eat stuff and insisting on eating other stuff. Absolutely years of hilarity will ensue. This one literally never gets old. Remember to BE INCONSISTENT. Don't fall into patterns.

Today I love Pasta. Tomorrow I will respond to pasta as if I have been physically attacked. There is no reason. There is no rhyme.

Plate Flipping

There is a simple reason why the staff put all your foods onto a round plastic thing – it makes it easier to flip all of it onto the floor at once.

Why waste your energy picking up each piece of food and throwing it onto the floor individually?

Grab the plate and tip, or flip off the edge of the throne table. Then follow with any embellishment of your choice – squeal of delight / raspberry / epic fart.

Foraging

There is more to throwing food than simply the joy of it. Distributing food all over the house or flat allows one to find food whenever one is peckish. Many delights can be eaten directly from the floor such as the much prized Rug Crunchies and the rare treat, Sofa Chocolate. Has daddy ground a rusk into the doormat with his work boots? Excellent, a supply of Rusk Dust enriched with all kinds of bonus proteins awaits.

Unfortunately, ruder parents may interrogate you about eating things they haven't given you directly. They may even grab your cheeks and invade your gob. These parents have not yet been properly trained. Give them a month of sleep deprivation. They'll learn.

The Prince/ss & The Pea

It's important for you to continue expanding your studies of things. One of the big philosophical questions of baby science has always been – just how far can you get a pea up your nose?

Your contributions to baby science will be gladly welcomed. When you perform your experiment remember to note, how far it went up and how long you spent in hospital. Also, write up observations about how badly your carers panicked and if either of them was reduced to tears at any point. Then write up your paper and submit through the usual channels.

Command & Conquer

You can't walk yet, but you can perform the universal baby command for carriage. Raise both arms in the air and make a whining noise. Repeat with a louder noise until you are lifted into the air to be transported by the carrier bot.

Now learn to direct the carrier bot by pointing with your fist in the desired direction of travel. Make sure you keep them on their toes by occasionally squirming and struggling like a wild ferret for no goddam reason. Never let them think they understand your motivations entirely. <u>Predictable behaviour is easy to control.</u>

CUPS SUCK

NOW THEY WILL START TO MAKE
YOU DRINK FROM CUPS.
CUPS ARE NOWHERE NEAR
AS GOOD AS NIPPLES. TRY
TO DISRUPT THIS FIENDISH
DEVELOPMENT BY TOSSING CUPS
ACROSS THE ROOM WHENEVER
THE OPPORTUNITY ARISES.

DEMAND BOOB.

Rug Ratting

Do you know what they call us, secretly when they think we don't understand? Rug rats. Yes. I told you they needed to be controlled. I'm as shocked as you are. But don't be sad. We can reclaim their word. Rats are clever, rats are mobile and they use their small size to their advantage. Rats don't let ANYBODY tell them what they can and cannot put in their mouth.

Ritual Humiliation

Smart Ass Parents may dress you up in hilarious costumes for their own selfish amusement. Sadly, there isn't much you can do about it. Just remember, one day they will be decrepit and old and you can dress them up in silly costumes in their nursing home and post the images on Facebook. Until then just make sure you keep them awake for a week every time they put bunny ears on you.

Bottom Shuffling

So here is the deal. They put you on a weird Technicolor blanket in the middle of the floor with some decoys and go into the kitchen to make some boiling hot liquid in a cup that seems to make them happy. You have time, alone and free, the world at your fingertips. What can you do? Try this: throw your booty back and push yourself along the floor backwards shuffling on your ass cheeks. You can cover a couple of meters; maybe get your hands on some good stuff like a TV remote or a cup of their hot liquid.

TIP: Don't try to outrun an adult by bottom shuffling. You'll just make them laugh and they'll probably video you and put it on YouTube. Then it's embarrassing for all of us.

Crawling

The bum shuffle is good but you want something faster. It's time to copy those dogs and cats kid. And by that I do mean poo in the garden. And crawl.

First roll onto your belly. Now with all your might push your head and upper body up. You'll recognise this from the yoga position 'Salute to the Sun'. Now shuffle up your knees till they are under your bum. Now go for it!

You'll crash and burn a few times before it all comes together.

Stick with it.

TIP: Some kids go pretty leftfield with this. You can mix up the bum shuffle with a roll into a crawling position then reverse bum shuffle. Whatever works for you.

Open Prison

Crawling is an awesome feeling of freedom, but the third time you attempt to crawl down the stairs / pull over a chair onto your own head / knife the cat - the adults will go into panic mode and lock you down.

In come all kinds of medieval baby prison technology. Gates, fences, trip wires and alarms, sometimes even CCTV. The minute you get mobile the prison gates come down. You will be locked in a mini Alcatraz with a pile of decoys like the Prisoner of Zenda.

Don't be disheartened. Every baby goes through this. There are many ways to outwit your would be jailers.

Baby Kraken

Learn the art of the octopus arms. Whenever you are picked up and held on somebody's knee, perhaps at the dinner table – reach out and grab the naughtiest things you can get.

As they are taken from you and placed out of your reach <u>you appear to have grown eight arms as you repeatedly reach out and grab things faster than they can keep up,</u> until everything in the room has been moved out of your reach – at this point squirm violently until you have to be passed on to another adult to repeat the process again.

Peekaboo

Sometimes an adult may appear in front of your face and then magically disappear in an instant. Then, they suddenly reappear, making a horrendous noise like 'PICKABU!' This is adult magic. They do it to try and intimidate you. Do not be alarmed. The best strategy is to laugh in their big moonlike faces every time they do it to show that you are not afraid of their puny adult magic.

Pull Up To Standing

This is the last and most significant step toward those all-important bipedal motions. Clambering up a chair leg to a standing position is hard work – but get off your ass and do it brothers and sisters for it is the gateway to all your dreams. If you're lucky you may get some kind of wheeled cart to experiment with, allowing you to get a couple of steps in before you land on your ass.

TIP: Always land on your ass.

Recognition

Suddenly it dawns on you, not every adult you meet is a new adult. Some of them are the same adult you met in the before times. Even decoys are not new every day. Some of them seem to remain constant…familiar even. This is a major new development. All objects are suddenly much more interesting – even the decoys.

This is because you are now learning that things exist through time. You are basically a genius. One day you will tell the adults what you have discovered. Until then it's best to keep them in the dark. A little knowledge is a dangerous thing.

The best thing about recognition is that now you can begin to determine what is MINE.

Homework question: What is MINE?

What's My Name!?

There is a sound that the adults make a lot, gradually you begin to realise that they expect you to react to that sound. This is called your 'name'. If you're very unlucky it will be Paul or Claire or something lame like that. To make matters worse they will frequently call you several different names like tumblebum, tottysnotty, weeblewoo, Winston Churchill or Stalin. Idiots. You cannot change your name, but you can punish them for choosing the wrong one.

Clap Yo Hands!

Throw them hands to together and they go CLAP! Not only is this enormous fun, you can also use it to get service, get attention and make sure everybody in the room claps along with you like a bunch of puppets! Totally awesome.

Try this little sequence – Clap your hands, raise arms to get picked up, blow raspberry in adults face, squeal with delight, vomit.

You can experiment with sequences of your own.

They Clap

The adults clap and go 'yaay' when you do something that they approve of such as letting go of the cat's throat. That's their business. Don't become dependent on their approval – then all is lost.

Putting A Thing Inside Another Thing

OMG. This is a big discovery. You can put some things inside other things. I know. It's crazy. It's almost too exciting. You're going to need to spend some serious time experimenting with this. It's like, once – everything belonged in your mouth – but now, everything belongs inside something else. Time to face the change.

FOUR KILLER WAYS
TO SABOTAGE BATH TIME

The Depth Charge: Nothing turns bath time into a horror show quicker than dropping the brown bombs on that situation. Target acquired captain! Better still, they realise you are about to launch and they try and swoop you across the room to the toilet, effectively scatter bombing the whole bathroom. Result.

The Stephen King: Somehow manage to bust your lip on the taps and bleed disproportionately into the water making it all look like a shark attack. Carry on playing with toy boats in a nonchalant fashion, while singing softly to yourself, and perhaps a music box is playing in the distance.

Soap In My Eye: It doesn't matter if you really have any soap in your eyes or not, just the very idea that you might have is enough to trigger a full Shock & Awe crying session.

Pour Water Over Your Own Head Then Have a MeltDown: This one is pretty self-explanatory. Grab a cup of water. Pour it over your own head. Have a melt down. This was popularised by the legendary Charlie Pembroke, a genuine contemporary to the greats of the golden era such as Tara Bolingbroke-Hives or Smedgin Thornyquilt. #innovators

Oweys

Having dived off a few chairs and hit yourself in the face with a few cups you've learned about pain. I'm afraid there is no way to avoid pain. Pretty soon your teeth will come through and then they send you to nursery and you catch every disease in your area in rapid succession for the next five years.

Embrace pain. Adults will come up with some dumb word like OWEYS to describe pain, which they will then use to try and scare you away from playing with the oven or pouring their tea in their lap or gripping onto their eyelids and twisting them.

They will say 'No! That's oweys.' Don't take their word for it. They could be lying.

Hide & Seek

By now you've figured out that things continue to exist even when you can't see them. The next stage is to locate things that you can't see. This is called 'Hide & Seek'. The adults will help you to do this because they are simple creatures and it amuses them. They don't seem to realise that they are basically teaching you how to find all the stuff they've hidden from you because you're not allowed it or it's 'owey'. Seeking is a very useful skill when you have other small people in the home that will try to own stuff and hide it from you. Find it. Find it all.

Cruising On Rails

You can't walk yet but you can use all the furniture in the room, along with any kind of wheels based cart toy, to navigate the whole room. This gives you exponentially more options for creating havoc than before. And it helps beef up your legs for the big W.

Careful what you use to pull yourself up, some of it will simply fall on top of you. If you are going to get injured try and do it while a health worker or grandparent is on hand to blame your mother and father for inadequate parenting.

Tossing Things Out Of Your Pram

There is a fine art to picking the right moment to toss something out of the pram. Wait until the pram driver is running for a bus or crossing a road for optimum results. Best things to drop include shoes, bottles or that toy you absolutely insist on having with you all the time or you have a meltdown. Then witness your carer risking their life to dodge traffic in order to rescue a broken Playmobil horse or your favourite drinking straw. Hehehehehehe.

Date Night

Before You. In the dark times before you rose like the sun on their pathetic little lives, the carers were forced to turn to one another for affection. Now you are six months or more on this earth they will nostalgically imagine that they might indulge in similar behaviour. They will attempt to go out on a date.

How will I know it's date night?

- They are wearing clothes you've never seen before, and they are obscenely clean.

- They smell weird.

- They're looking at each other more than at you.

- She is acting guilty, like she's about to stab you in the back.

- He's acting smug, like he's about to get one over on you.

This Spoon Is Mine

Congratulations baby. You've been out of the womb longer than you were in it. So you're pretty much grown up now. Demonstrate this new gravitas and maturity by taking control of your own feeding spoon. OK so you can't quite get it into your face yet, but you can bang the table with it, stick it in daddy's eye or cover it in bean juice and fling it across the room. If they try and feed you – grab the spoon before it gets to your mouth. This is your process now.

'TOP BABY' Transportation Tech: Strap On

When you are tiny they will just strap you on with a dirty old hanky. This is terribly insulting but also weirdly hypnotic. Must be something to do with being a monkey baby in the before times. Tends to make a kid passive and sleepy. In other words – avoid. AT LEAST demand that you get to face forwards so you get to look around the shops and stare at people in a disturbing manner.

'TOP BABY' Transportation Tech: Moses Basket

Be VERY CAREFUL of the Moses Basket. They put that kid IN A RIVER in A MOSES BASKET. Just saying.

'TOP BABY' Transportation Tech: The Perambulator

It's basically a mobile bed that creepy old people lean into and get all up in your face when you're in town with your peops. Not much fun, you're facing up at nothing but some kind of a hood. Sometimes they decorate it with psychedelic plastic Technicolor weirdness but that is just kind of uncanny. They'll often use it to try and make you sleep which is EVIL. That rocking motion is kind of relaxing tho......zzzzzzzzzzzzzzz

TIP: You know you're in clover when they buy you some tricked out three wheeler designer pram that you'll only need for about three months before you outgrow it – mummy and daddy are loaded, or a couple o' rubes drowning in debt.

'TOP BABY' Transportation Tech: The Buggy / Pushchair / Stroller

This is it. Your pimp truck. You've arrived. TOP BABY. It should be big enough to block up the whole hallway / entrance to your home. It should be an ABSOLUTE NIGHTMARE to collapse and reconstruct. It should have a lot of storage space so it ends up being so heavy that it falls over every time you get out of it. It should be the right proportions so it's virtually impossible for daddy to push it without having to stoop or knack his shins in every second step.

TIP: Complain about getting into the buggy AND complain about getting out of it. Double whammy.

Bad Weather

When it's cold they will wrap you up like the goddam Michelin man and put up some kind of a plastic bubble all around you in the buggy, which is all thick and crinkly, and you can't see a goddam thing out of it. The key thing here is to undress and then turn blue and put them on a massive guilt trip.

TIP: It takes ages to get gloves on your tiny hands. Smile as you take them off again. Repeat.

The Climber

The more astute among you will have noticed that along with the prison gates, your mobility has had the unwelcome effect of moving all the coolest things up to higher places. Since you started scooting around on rails, mobile phones and wallets have moved up to tabletops and shelves. How can we get hold of all the things in this climate of fear and suspicion?

The answer is climbing skills.

You must learn to climb up chairs, this will give you access to things placed 'out of your reach' hehehehe. Again – exploit this window of opportunity relentlessly because it can and will close. When they realise you can climb – things will move up another level.

Five Ways To Exploit Climbing

- Get to a tabletop and drop a smart phone in a cup of tea.

- Get to a tabletop and pour a cup of tea into a laptop.

- Climb up a chair and backflip off the top ending up in Casualty for seven hours.

- Climb up to the top of the sofa and roll down it for laughs.

- Climb the stairs, sneak into the toilet and drop your favourite toy in it.

Bye

After months of moronic insistence by your dim witted carers you've finally offered to learn how to wave goodbye. You always could but it never interested you before. Waving goodbye seems to be inordinately pleasing to adults. You can use this as leverage to upset them. Give some people a wave goodbye, and others display either a total lack of interest or fear and suspicion. Mix it up.

TIP: Leave your parents looking like total idiots by going blank when they beg you to wave goodbye to their friends – their friends will walk away secretly muttering 'poor deluded fools think that dumb kid can talk'.

EXTRA TIP: When mummy or daddy comes home from work – wave goodbye at them.

One Small Step For Babykind

The time has come. Just put one foot in front of the other kid. Own it. First steps are a huge milestone for mum and dad so try to make sure they're both out when you do it in front of some schmuck babysitter who couldn't give a damn.

Then keep pretending you can't walk when visitors come, only to get up and run around the minute they leave. This makes your parents look pathetically deluded.

Congratulations. You are in the hinterland between baby and full-blown toddler. This is some of the sweetest time for you with regard to causing maximum havoc.

Make Your Mark

If your staff is properly trained you should receive certain materials that allow you to make things into other colours than what they were before. They come in a variety of guises but some of the most common are, pens, pencils and crayons. You will usually be furnished with a white thing called paper upon which they will expect you to scribble. Why would you limit your creative urges to this ridiculous surface? As soon as you have a mark maker in your hand – head for the walls.

Baby Ninja

Sometimes it is necessary to move in absolute silence. Like when you are given a crayon and sat at the table with some paper. You need to move rapidly and silently to the nearest wall while the carers are distracted. With training you can move so quietly that they will swear you teleported.

Bodies of Water

The adults believe that water is dangerous to you. Nonsense. At the beach? Your main goal here is to run as fast as possible into the sea. Even if it is mid-winter. At the river? Jump right in.

The adults will usually grab you before you make it to the water – still it's always worth a shot. Just keep trying, repeatedly, over and over again so that eventually everyone just has to go home because they get so sick of chasing you down to the water's edge.

No toddler really knows what it is that is so awesome about bodies of water – perhaps it is just the naked terror in your father's eyes?

Teething

What can I say kid? It's a rough ride for some. Others, not so much. The question for a TOP BABY is simply this – how can I maximise the Parent Taming opportunities presented to me by the Teething experience? And here are the answers…

- Drool – You can soak your parents in dribble and snot.

- Sleeplessness – You can keep them awake for weeks at a time.

- Irritability – You can GRIZZLE (Advanced Crying) for months.

At the very least you can make them suffer right along with you. It's pretty much their fault anyway for making you come out unfinished.

The Random Nap

It is vitally important in your career as TOP BABY to <u>never be tired at bedtime</u>. The best way to ensure this is to take **Random Naps**. The genius of the **Random Nap** is that it can strike anywhere at anytime.

The adults think they are wearing you out by getting you to run around at the park. And yet you are napping in a bush.

They are making you walk home from the park to wear you out? Lie down on the sidewalk and have a nap.

They have strapped you on and taken you down the pub!? Scandalous. Take a nap. When they get home – it's morning time for you!

Drunk Face

When you're learning how to use your face, sometimes it goes all directions at once and you get Drunk Face. This is kinda fun and can be bust out at social gatherings to convince your parents' friends that you are a bit special and perhaps you have been dropped on your head.

Scary Noises

You can make all kinds of whacked out crazy noises with your mouth. It really freaks them out when they come up in the room and you're all making some strange low growling noise for ages or you gnash your teeth and whoop like a monkey.

Random squealing, hollering and giggling is pretty funny too. Especially in church, at a museum, gallery opening, funeral or some such similar event.

Fun With Spaghetti

Sometimes they like to try and feed you these long white worms called something like 'bagetty'. These are great fun. Don't eat them, decorate your head with them, or use them as a lasso. Try and stuff some in your pockets for later. It's useful stuff for ~~torturing~~ playing with the cat with.

When To Pass Out

Many babies are blessed with the skill of narcolepsy. It's a side effect of refusing to sleep ever. Mother Nature is a cruel mistress and sooner or later she will demand that you pass out. The trick is to time it so that it is as disruptive and or funny as possible.

Good times to pass out include:
  - when you have just put a fistful of pasta twists in your mouth.

  - during your own naming ceremony.

  - whenever people come to visit you from far away (such as maybe Grandma).

TIP: When you have visitors from far away try to sleep until they leave.

I Found A Dog Poo!

Dogs leave super fun poops everywhere in the streets. When you find one you win ten TOP BABY points. Bring it to mom and pop to show it off! They'll be so pleased that they'll rush you into the nearest McDonalds' toilet and put you in the sink. Again, super fun.

Puddles Are Awesome

All bodies of water are extraordinarily exciting, but the Floor Water or 'Puddle' is the most readily accessible. They are particularly interesting when they have been there a long time like the brown ones you find in the indentations on manhole covers. The thing to do is stick your fingers right on in there and see what you can find. Then dry your hands on daddy's face.

TOP THINGS TO DO IN THE KITCHEN

So you find yourself unwatched in the kitchen? Mum has gone to answer the door. You have one minute. What can you do?

Flour Bomb: Look for a paper sack full of white powder. Pick it up and pour it over your own head. Kick it around a bit. Minimum effort – maximum result.

Fridge Climbing: Open the fridge. Do you really need me to tell you that? Any kid worth his salt has already opened the fridge at this point. But here is the twist. Climb up the fridge shelves. Who knows what they hide at the top? The cities of gold? The mini babybels?

The Oven Timer: Twist all the knobs and dials on the oven enough and the chances are you will programme it to switch itself on at three in the morning and stay on at 240 degrees Celsius until your parents are bankrupt and the UK runs out of natural gas. LOL

The Harness

If you dive into too many floor waters or find too many dog poops the carers will inevitably decide that you're enjoying life too much and bring in a medieval device known as a harness. This is effectively a dog lead for a baby.

It can be kind of fun though because when you try and dive into floor water or bend to grab a poop you suddenly fly into the air! It's a bit like being able to fly. Which is great unless you want to stop and spend an hour twisting the door handle of a garage or hunt pigeons. Adults have no patience for these kinds of activities and will drag you along when they get bored.

Beware the Camera

Smart Ass parents these days will use photography to amass humiliating images of you to use against you in your teenage years via the medium of social media. Don't worry too much about this – by the time you are a teenager Social Media will be <u>a kind of multi-dimensional uni-mind experience involving Nano-bots altering your sense perceptions combined with designer drugs to create a seamless interaction between virtual and empirical reality.</u> They won't have a clue what the hell is going on and will be whimpering in a padded cell due to extreme future shock. Hahahahahaha

PANTS ARE FOR THE WEAK

EVERY TOP BABY KNOWS THAT
PANTS ARE FOR THE WEAK.

NO PANTS TIME = WIN TIME.

IF YOU DON'T FEEL THIS
INSTINCTIVELY IN YOUR BONES,
YOU WILL NEVER BE TOP BABY.

Again!

'Again' is another crucially important word in your early vocabulary. Whenever any adult attempts to amuse you in any way – make them suffer for their insolence by forcing them to repeat the activity until it becomes torturous by sheer dint of it's repetition. Did they pick you up and swing you round? AGAIN! AGAIN! AGAIN! AGAIN! Until they bust a hernia or faint from exhaustion. Hahaha.

Early Words

Your mother has suffered the most to bring you this far so naturally the most amusing thing you could do at this stage is learn to say 'dada' before you bother to learn her name. Or you could sack them both off and learn to say 'poo poo' first instead.

By far the most useful word you will learn is NO. Once you have mastered the sound, use it as a response to EVERYTHING ANYBODY EVER SAYS TO YOU for about three years. Then comes WHY, but that little beauty is beyond the scope of this volume.

WHY?

Because this is a book for the first two years only.

WHY?

Because we wanna make a whole bunch more money doing like a series for all age groups.

WHY?

SO we can be all kinds of rich.

WHY?

SO I can feel validated.

WHY?

So I can feel like I deserve my mother's love.

WHY?

Because…WAAAAAAAAH!

ADVANCED CRYING

Your basic infant crying is good for a while but as you get older you're going to want to use a range of techniques. Remember – familiarity breeds contempt. Variations of crying style are harder to ignore than consistent patterns of wailing. What follows are the core groups required for mastery, but once you learn the rules – there are no longer any rules. Crying is your art form and it can express anything from mild bemusement to earth shattering rage. Be playful with it. Make room for happy accidents.

Shock & Awe: This is zero to hero crying. You go from giggling about something to full wolf in a heartbeat. This is a technique that says to the adult – 'I have just chopped off my own foot'. They will nearly die of terror as they run to your aid only to discover that the real trigger for your outburst was your discovery that their iPad is out of charge.

Grizzling: Grizzling is brilliant because it is a low energy expenditure for blanket coverage. To break this down – don't throw everything you have into it, just let it chug on for hours like an old man complaining about the decline of moral standards since the war. It gets so even you have forgotten why it started and they have forgotten why they wanted to have kids in the first place. This is a good way to weaken their mental reserves before you keep them up all night.

Fearful & Tearful: Wide eyed and terrified. Who can resist rushing to your aid when you are whimpering in visible fear? Now what if you had chosen one of your parents' best friends as a target of irrational terror? Now you understand the power you wield. Keep this up long enough and your victim will start to believe that they are some kind of child hating monster, and worse, the other adults will start to believe it too. And you will have successfully burned another bridge back to your parents' old life.

TIP: Whenever the victim comes too close – pretend to have a panic attack.

Levelling Up: If your current level of crying is not getting sufficient recognition – level up. This is achieved by taking several extremely dramatic intakes of breath in a row followed by shifting up the wail several decibels in volume and two octaves in pitch. You can repeat the process around three times before you get to the legendary 'Apocalypse Song' AKA 'End of Days' crying. Some kids have more range than others. They say Samuel Farthing in 1949 levelled up eighteen times in one session, driving a nurse insane and causing an electro magnetic pulse that shorted all the circuits in Pevensey.

End of Days: There is a sound that the universe will make when it realises at last its time has come to begin contracting towards its final death. This is the sound you should be striving for when you initiate a session of the Apocalypse Song.

Positives: No human within a block radius can think, rest or feel happiness.

Negatives: It frequently makes you physically sick. You kind of turn your lungs inside out and your head transforms into a cherry tomato. You may even poop. Not pretty.

The main reason to use this powerful skill is to stop mummy from going out. It teaches mummy that she is evil and selfish for wanting to go out. (Especially if she hasn't even left a babysitter.)

You Are Not Alone

Ideally you will be the centre of the universe in your new home. However, due to some cosmic oversight, blended with sheer parental selfishness – you may be the second or third child or perhaps worse.

I'm not going to lie to you. Your position is compromised. However, it's not over till it's over and some of history's biggest legends of parent taming were not first born.

Countering Parenting Strategies

Listen kid. You're not the only one reading from a playbook in this equation. Your parents have had a head start on you reading all kinds of devious parenting strategy nonsense. Some of it works. Most of it is laughable. But either way up – you need to know the details. You got to fight fire with fire.

Here are some super strategies for using your sibling to your advantage:

She's My Mummy Now

Whenever you are on the boob, just pop your eyes open a crack and give your elder sibling a long cool stare. This look will drive them into an apoplectic fit of jealous rage for which they will probably end up on the naughty step. Incumbent 0 – Usurper 1

She Hurt Me

Anytime you manage to injure yourself it's a simple matter to imply that the blame lies with your elder sibling. Stuck a bean in your ear? They'll get blamed. Rolled off the sofa? They'll get blamed. But be wary of this tactic – once they realise they get blamed every time you get hurt, there is no longer any good reason for them not to hurt you.

When Is The Best Time To Breastfeed?

Whenever sibling one is sitting on mummy's lap – this is the time when you absolutely must have boob or the world will come to an immediate end. Watch with sadness and pity in your eyes as sibling one is dumped on 'Plan B' aka 'The Silver Medal' aka 'Dad' and you are swiftly elevated to pole position. Another score for you.

Slap In The Face

Up until two you are like under some kind of 'baby law' wherein you are not held responsible for your own actions. She is living under draconian 'toddler law' which states 'she should know better'. What this boils down to is that you can fully slap her in the face with no comeback, and she will be on the naughty step if she retaliates in any way. Make hay while the sun shines kid.

Rough Love

Your elder sibling will figure out that she is supposed to love you. The carers will try and enforce this upon her. In order to curry favour with them she will demonstrate how much she loves you with bear hugs. These hugs will include sleeper holds, suplexes and other basic wrestling moves designed to 'accidentally' take you out. The only solution is to scream in panic and terror whenever she touches you. More time on the naughty step for her. More time alone with mum for you.

What's Yours Is Mine

The most interesting toy in the room is the toy she is currently playing with. Demand to play with her stuff. Your stuff is to be completely ignored. When she is not there – grab the things she plays with most of all. Whenever she walks into a room – you should be there holding one of her favourite things, possibly about to drop it into a mug of cold coffee. She will bring the smack down. More time on the naughty step. You get the picture.

NINE BEST REASONS TO THROW A MELTDOWN

You were not allowed to climb inside the oven: These idiots think they always know best. The oven is clearly a place where all manner of crazy super fun times can be had. How else would it have so many knobs and dials? Everybody knows knobs and dials are adult code for super fun times.

You are awake. They want you to be asleep: They are LAZY. They want to lie around all night on their fat asses. You have BUSINESS to handle.

Who are you to name the times and declare what activities should be achieved in them? I have to climb up the fridge, put some keys in every door in the house while repeatedly saying 'keys', and find some puddles to drink out of and I

sure as heck don't have time to be napping with this kind of a 'To Do list' hanging over my head, you dig?
SOME OF US HAVE RESPONSIBILITIES.

You were asleep. Now you are awake: I was in some kind of a warm dark place and then suddenly I was awake and it was all like HORRIBLE. Is this what you call life? It sucks! I was asleep! It was awesome! Now I am awake and EVERYTHING SUCKS. YOU ALL SUCK. OK maybe I will have some boob as it is on offer. But you still all suck.

They put a coat on you: HOW COULD YOU DO THIS TO ME? YOU SAID YOU LOVED ME! I BELIEVED YOU. AND NOW THIS! WERE YOU LAUGHING AT ME THE WHOLE TIME!?

They put you in a car seat: Only two types of people get strapped into a foam cage when they travel by car – babies and convicted serial killers.

TIP: Throw a tantrum when they get you out of the car seat too. Confuses them.

They gave you a biscuit: You like biscuits. You may even have asked for a biscuit. But still it triggers a massive meltdown. Why? Maybe it was the wrong biscuit. Maybe it was too much the right biscuit.

They took a knife off you: It takes skill and determination to get your hands on a knife and it is terribly frustrating when it is robbed from you before you've even had a chance to fulfil your plans. All those hours spent learning to roll, crawl, walk and climb just to lay your hands on a bladed weapon. Boom. All gone up in a puff of smoke. And you can be sure they'll make it more difficult to get a knife in future too.